BEST JOB SEARCH
TIPS FOR AGE

A PRACTICAL WORK OPTIONS RESOURCE FOR

BABY BOOMERS

TOBY HABERKORN & ELIZABETH O'NEAL

Although every precaution has been taken to verify the accuracy of the information contained herein, the authors and publisher assume no responsibility for any errors or omissions. No liability is assumed for damages that may result from the use of this information.

Published by Baypointe Publishers

Authors may be contacted at http://tobyhaberkorn.com/

ISBN: 978-0-9916236-4-8 Paperback

ISBN: 978-0-9916236-5-5 E-book

Library of Congress Control Number: 2016919004

1. Layoff 2. Fired 3. Age Discrimination 4. Networking 5. Job Interviews 6. Salary Negotiations 7. Resumes 8. Retirement. 9. Consultant/Freelance 10. Contractor 11. Part-time 12. Entrepreneur 13. Volunteer 14. Success

Summary: This book provides job search advice and numerous resources for Baby Boomers seeking paid employment and/or volunteer work.

Book and Cover design by Giulia Luca

ACKNOWLEDGEMENTS

Thank you to all who contributed to making this book a resource for anyone who wants to continue to work past age 60. We are grateful to our beta readers who gave us their time and input. Special appreciation to our families who patiently watched us develop **Best Job Search Tips For Age 60-Plus: A Practical Work Options Resource For Baby Boomers** *from concept to reality.*

TOBY HABERKORN & ELIZABETH O'NEAL

TABLE OF
CONTENTS

CHAPTER 6

CHAPTER 7

"Your most important work
is always ahead of you, never
behind you."

STEPHEN COVEY

"The boomers' biggest impact will be on eliminating the term 'retirement' and inventing a new stage of life... the new career arc."

— ROSABETH MOSS KANTER

CHAPTER 1

Decisions—What are your Options?

Welcome to *Best Job Search Tips For Age 60-Plus: A Practical Work Options Resource For Baby Boomers* where you will learn about realistic work options and job search strategies available to you today.

For many Baby Boomers over age 60, continuing to work is an important decision requiring careful evaluation. Perhaps you've been laid off and are considering whether or not to conduct a search for a new job at all. Or perhaps you no longer enjoy your current job and are tired of punching the clock. You may be unsure about what work possibilities exist and would like to learn more about these opportunities, including consulting, freelance, contract, part-time, volunteer positions, and even becoming an entrepreneur.

Due to layoffs, mergers and other circumstances, many of you retirement-eligible Baby Boomers probably no longer expect to climb the corporate ladder or become "Employee of the Year," and recognize that your income may decline. But you may still want to remain in the game, contributing to an organization and earning some money.

⇜➡ Factors that may influence your decision:

- Do you need to continue working for income?

- Have you enjoyed your career and want to continue working in your field? If so, can you perform this role as a consultant or contractor or work on a project-by-project basis?

- Do you have the resources available to allow for learning something new? Does this new area require going to school, getting a certification or specific training?

- Before you return to school, carefully consider the cost of additional education or training. Is the return on investment worthwhile?

- Are you afraid to stop working because you can't imagine retirement and are worried about how to fill your days without a job?

Tips

✓ Talk with a financial planner to clearly understand your financial position. What are your expected expenses and how much income do you need?

✓ Research your Social Security and Medicare options. When is the best time for you to file with the government for benefits?

✓ How much money will you realistically need to maintain your lifestyle? Based on this information, you can determine whether you must work full-time or part-time or whether volunteering will do.

✓ Reflect on and determine what's important to you now. Set goals for the next two years.

Resources

 The Intern
A film starring Robert De Niro as a frustrated Boomer in a millennials' workplace.

 "60 Ways to Find Meaning In Life After 60"
http://www.huffingtonpost.com/margaret-manning/60-ways-to-find-meaning-i_b_5306222.html

 "60 Years Old with Zero Retirement Savings"
http://www.daveramsey.com/blog/60-years-old-zero-retirement

 "How to Change Your Life at 60"
http://www.theguardian.com/society/2012/jun/04/change-your-life-at-60

 "Laid Off at 60: What To Do Next"
http://www.nextavenue.org/laid-60-what-do-next

 Social Security Administration
http://www.ssa.gov

 Medicare
http://www.medicare.gov

Notes

"In the middle of difficulty lies opportunity."

— ALBERT EINSTEIN

CHAPTER 2

Twenty-First Century Job Search

Job security doesn't exist anymore. Changes to the economic and business climate mean most people have had multiple employers and positions during their careers. This is the "new normal."

The GOOD NEWS is that people are living into their nineties, so age 60-plus is barely past the mid-point of their adult lives. Although Boomers are and will be retiring, many employers fear the "silver tsunami" of highly qualified retirement-eligible workers leaving their companies. In some industries, a knowledge vacuum already exists because employers did not recruit critical career specialties during difficult economic times. These employers are now offering incentives to these highly valued employees to remain in the workforce.

So, you wonder, how could these employed Boomers affect your situation? With many Boomers remaining in the workplace, the working age has stretched beyond age 60-plus.

While it's true that most employers want to hire the 35-40 year old superstar, these superstars are a scarce commodity and employers regularly hire other qualified workers who don't fit this ideal profile.

Employers who hire Boomers find that they are productive and add considerable value to the company but when the employment market is tight, society and employers often fall back on false stereotypes: Boomers are too old, too slow, too inflexible or that they're technologically ignorant and resistant to innovation.

You can neutralize these negatives and get a job by using the tips in this book. After all, the Alpha or oldest Boomers have already changed many of the stereotypes our society holds. Most Boomers would say they are very different from their parents, who appeared to be much older at the same age and saw retirement as the reward for their years of work.

Even with sharp minds and good health, many Boomers are surprised to see their aging reflections in the mirror. Just as Boomer bodies change, so has the workplace. Your ability to adapt is vital to getting hired and supporting your personal growth.

Some of you may remember the old-time job search methods of reading the newspaper classifieds and applying for the advertised positions. This approach does not work today. A successful twenty-first century job search will require you to learn the most up-to-date methods.

⏱ How long will it take me to land a new job?

- The shortest job search will generally be for the same role in your current industry.

- If you change roles or industries, your job search may take more time.

- Generally you should expect to spend one to two months searching for every $10,000 of your targeted salary.

Tips

✓ Get involved in your industry and community by joining specific professional groups and your industry association.

✓ Learn new or expand existing skills for the workplace. Check for free online courses.

✓ If currently employed, consider switching to a position that may be more marketable (e.g. from management to a staff role.)

Resources

 Free Learning Websites:

- **Coursera** *http://www.coursera.org*
  Provides universal access to the world's best education, partnering with top universities and organizations to offer courses online.

- **GCF Learn Free** *http://www.gcflearnfree.org*
  Offers free online classes in technology and other subjects.

- **Khan Academy** *http://www.khanacademy.org*
  Provides a free, world-class education for anyone, anywhere.

- **Techboomers** *http://techboomers.com*
  Teaches mature adults and other inexperienced Internet users with basic computer skills about websites that can help improve their quality of life.

 Career One Stop
http://www.careeronestop.org/resourcesfor/olderworker/older-worker.aspx
Provides advice and resources for the mature worker.

 Encore *http://www.encore.org*
Taps the skills and experience of those in midlife and older to improve communities and the world.

National Older Worker Career Center
http://www.nowcc.org
Partners with the Natural Resources Conservation
Service to place experienced workers into positions
supporting conservation and environmental
protection efforts.

 Over 50 Job Board *http://www.over50jobboard.com*
Lists jobs for over-50 workers, with postings
for part-time and full-time positions in specific
industries.

 Senior Job Bank *http://www.seniorjobbank.org*
Provides job listings and career information for
seniors.

 Workforce50 *http://www.workforce50.com*
Posts jobs for older workers and resources for midlife
career changes.

Notes

_____

_____

_____

_____

_____

_____

_____

_____

_____

_____

_____

_____

_____

_____

_____

_____

_____

_____

"Flexibility requires an open mind and a welcoming of new alternatives."

—DEBORAH DAY

CHAPTER 3

Alternative Work Options: Consultant, Freelancer, Contractor, Part-Timer, and Entrepreneur

Section 3.1 - Consultant or Freelancer

Let's review alternative work options such as consulting and freelancing.

A consultant is defined as an expert who advises individuals and companies. Consultants are paid to provide solutions. They identify problems, offer objective opinions, train employees and stimulate change. Your expertise and ability to implement solutions will be an important factor in building a successful consultancy.

Sometimes it's hard to tell the difference between consultants and freelancers. Freelancers are frequently hired for short-term assignments and may also work on multiple projects for several clients. Both consultants and freelancers must network and market their skills. They typically do not receive benefits and are responsible for reporting their own taxes.

⬆⬆ Advantages of consulting or freelancing:

- You can concentrate on work content and deliverables for different projects.

- You can work for a variety of employers.

- You are self-employed.

- You can determine your own schedule and hourly or project rates.

- You may gain tax advantages.

⑦ If you are considering becoming a consultant or freelancer, answer these questions:

- Do you have an area of expertise?

- Do you have expertise clients would pay for?

- Do you need additional training, certifications and/or special licensing?

- Do you have the resources necessary to set up an office, whether home-based or leased?

- Do you have the organizational skills to work effectively and independently?

- Do you have an existing network or do you need to develop one?

🤝 How do you find clients?

- Research what types of clients use your services.

- Research your competitors.

- Join and network within relevant groups and professional societies.

- Become active on social media such as LinkedIn, the premier networking site for business professionals.

- Participate in high-potential LinkedIn client-type groups and become visible by posting targeted information regularly and participating in discussion forums. *(See Section 5.4 for more information on social media.)*

- Create a business plan that clarifies your marketing and personal goals.

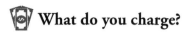 **What do you charge?**

There are several approaches to determining your consulting rates. Remember your fees must include your overhead expenses as well as any other costs.

- Research the competition and charge a similar fee.

- Triple your workplace hourly rate for a consulting hourly rate.

- To derive a daily rate, multiply your consulting hourly rate by an eight-hour day.

- Set a consulting fee for specific projects by determining the number of hours you will allocate to this work.

POTENTIAL CONSULTING BUSINESSES

Accounting	Graphic Design
Appraisals	Grant Writing
Auditing	Insurance
Business Writing/Editing	Interior Design
Coaching (business, career, life)	Learning and Development Training
College/Private School Admissions	Logistics/Moving
Communications	Marketing
Computer Services/Software Applications	Online Research
Education/Testing	Photography
Eldercare	Public Relations
Engineering	Publishing
Estate Sales	Real Estate Management
Executive search/Recruiting	Social Media Services
Financial Planning	Virtual Assistance
Fundraising	Website Development

Tips

✓ Discuss the venture with your spouse, partner, family and friends.

✓ Determine whether you will need professional liability insurance.

Resources

 "7 Steps to Starting Your Own Business Over 50"
http://www.grandparents.com/money-and-work/career/
steps-starting-business

 "8 Steps to Becoming a Consultant"
http://www.sba.gov/blogs/8-steps-becoming-consultant-50

 American Association of Retired Persons (AARP)
http://www.aarp.org/work/job-hunting/info-06-2009/
job_search_resources.html
Provides a variety of information for seniors, including employment and job search for ages
50-plus.

 Association of Accredited Small Business Consultants *http://www.aasbc.com*
Trains and certifies SME (small business and small-to-medium enterprise) consultants.

 Association of Professional Communications Consultants *http://consultingsuccess.org/wp*
Helps new consultants enter the communication consulting profession and experienced consultants enhance and grow their businesses.

Independent Computer Consultant Association
http://www.icca.org
Assists small computer-consulting businesses in the
United States.

 Institute of Management Consultants USA
http://www.imcusa.org
Promotes excellence and ethics in management
consulting through certification, education and
professional resources.

 Service Corps of Retired Executives (SCORE)
http://www.score.org
Helps small businesses get off the ground, grow and
achieve their goals through education and mentorship.

 Small Business Administration (SBA)
http://www.sba.gov
Provides support to entrepreneurs and small
businesses.

Section 3.2 – Contractor

As a Boomer, you already know that job security is uncertain, so contracting may be just the ticket for you. Today, companies use contractors who frequently are in the 60-plus age range. **Many employers are quite receptive to working with Boomers on a contractual basis.** Contractors are not company employees. Employers usually engage them in **full-time** or **part-time** capacities for an extended or specific period. They are paid by the hour and do not receive employee benefits from the company. Contractors can independently contract themselves or go through an agency which may offer benefits. They or their contracting agency are responsible for reporting all taxes.

↑↑ Advantages of contracting:

- You can concentrate on work content and deliverables.

- You may attend fewer meetings.

- You can often avoid office politics.

- You are able to work for a variety of employers and assignments.

- You have the possibility of flexible hours.

- You may receive overtime.

- You may gain tax advantages.

(?) If you are considering becoming a contractor, answer these questions:

- Do you have a marketable area of expertise?

- Can you work independently and organize yourself to be effective?

- Can you make the transition from your former role as a full-time employee with benefits to a contractor position?

How do you find work?

- Research what types of companies use your services.

- Research your competitors.

- Sign up with staffing companies that contract out employees.

- Review and apply for positions and projects through appropriate companies and targeted websites.

- Join and network within relevant groups and professional societies for referrals.

- Participate in high-potential LinkedIn client-type groups and become visible by posting targeted information regularly and participating in discussion forums. *(See Section 5.4 for more information on social media.)*

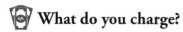 What do you charge?

- Contractors are usually offered an hourly rate by the hiring company but may be able to negotiate the amount.

- Contractors frequently receive higher hourly rates than employees because no benefits are included in the compensation.

Section 3.3 - Part-Timer

Do you want to continue to work, but not in a full-time role? If so, part-time work may be for you. Working less than 35 hours a week is considered part-time.

If you want a work life that allows you to have time and energy to explore other interests, then it's worth thinking about how your previous experience may translate into a part-time job or project-based work.

As with any other type of job, part-time work requires market research to determine what industries need your skills on a part-time basis. Do you already have or do you need to develop contacts to reach the hiring authority? If you're not confident you can approach companies directly with your skills and expertise, you may want to consider signing on with a staffing company that is responsible for placing its clients into part-time positions.

↑↑ Advantages of part-time work:

- You are making some income.

- You have less pressure from your job.

- You have a more flexible schedule.

- You have time to pursue other interests.

- You can save money on transportation, meals and other costs associated with working full-time.

⑦ If you are considering becoming a part-timer, answer these questions to determine your best options:

- How much work income do you need?

- Do you want a position with significant responsibilities or a "no muss, no fuss" job?

🤝 How do you find part-time work?

Job searches for part-time positions are similar to searches for full-time jobs.

- Research businesses (service, retail, sales, technical specialties, etc.) that hire part-timers.

- Find businesses that require your skills.

- Target companies or organizations by using online resources.

- Use job bank websites where job seekers can search and apply for job openings online.

- Network with people online and in-person about your part-time job quest.

- Select companies that are a reasonable commute from your location.

What type of compensation can you expect?

- Research the pay ranges for your part-time position.

- Negotiate your salary or hourly rate whenever possible.

PART-TIME JOBS	
Accounting	Inside Sales
Adjunct Instructor	Insurance Sales
Bagger	Interior Designer
Barista	Information Technology
Bartender	Library Assistant
Bookkeeper	Mail Guest Services
Brand Ambassador	Mediator
Cashier	Movie Theater jobs
Catering	Online Product Reviewer
Childcare	Sales
Coaching	Tax Preparer
Concierge	Teacher
Customer Service Desk	Tour Guide
Engineering	Travel Agent
Front Desk Clerk-hotel	Tutor
Graphic Artist	Weekend Receptionist

Tips

✓ Decide what type of part-time job you want.

✓ Consider your work experience and interests to discover skills that could turn into a part-time job.

✓ Spread the word that you are looking for a part-time job by contacting groups which include your personal, professional and social networks.

Resources

Fiverr *http://www.fiverr.com*
An online global marketplace where freelancers offer services starting at $5 per job performed.

FlexJobs *http://www.flexjobs.com*
A site which lists telecommuting, part-time and flexible jobs throughout the USA.

Freelance.com *http://www.freelance.com*
A large marketplace which connects employers (often major corporate accounts) with freelance service providers or very small companies.

Guru *http://www.guru.com/d/jobs*
An online international network where freelancers offer their technical, creative or business services to individuals and companies.

Indeed.com *http://www.indeed.com/q-Independent-Contractor-jobs.html*
One of the largest job postings sites.

Peopleperhour *http://peopleperhour.com*
A marketplace connecting small businesses and freelancers.

Ratracerebellion *http://ratracerebellion.com*
A resource for work at home jobs.

SimplyHired
http://www.simplyhired.com/search?q=contractor
A large database for a variety of job postings.

SnagaJob *http://www.snagajob.com/*
A job bank for hourly positions.

Staffing Companies In Your City
http://www.bestofstaffing.com
A list of staffing companies throughout the U.S.

UpWork *http://www.upwork.com*
A global platform where businesses and independent professionals connect remotely.

Working Couples Jobs *http://workingcouples.com/*
A site that specifically posts positions for couples.

Section 3.4 - Entrepreneur

Perhaps you are ready to call the shots yourself. If so, you may want to consider becoming an entrepreneur.

Entrepreneurs are individuals who want to work for themselves rather than as an employee. They start their own businesses—frequently based on their previous work experience, interests, or hobbies—and assume all of the risks and rewards.

Franchises

Buying a franchise of an already established business is another way to become an entrepreneur. In return for a fee, individuals purchase the right to use someone else's proven successful business system. They sign a franchise agreement which spells out the franchisor and franchisee responsibilities for operating the business.

Depending on the contractual agreement, franchisors may provide help with site selection and development, initial and ongoing training, marketing and guidance. All franchises require financial investment depending on the size and scope of the business. The franchisor, Small Business Administration and other institutions may offer financing.

Low-Investment Entrepreneurial Ventures

You may be intrigued by the idea of starting a new venture requiring little capital. If so, building a hobby into an income producing business may be a good option for you. Relatively low-cost businesses, mostly in the service sector, include event planner, pet sitter, web site developer, physical trainer, etc. You can find more information about low-investment entrepreneurial ventures in the Appendices under Profiles.

⬆⬆ Advantages of being an entrepreneur:

- You choose your opportunity.
- You enjoy the excitement of growing a business.
- You are the boss and make the decisions.
- You have the ultimate responsibility for your undertaking.

⑦ If you are considering becoming an entrepreneur, answer these questions:

- Do you have a burning desire to be your own boss?
- Do you have a passion for a specific type of business?
- Do you have the financial resources to invest in a startup business or franchise?
- Can you take a calculated financial risk?
- Can you afford to lose your investment? What about your retirement savings?

- Are you prepared to create and follow a detailed business plan?

- Are you a self-starter and realistically optimistic?

- Do you have the energy, endurance and health to work for as long as it takes to achieve business success?

- What about your lifestyle, family and other interests? Are you willing to devote all your efforts toward your business?

- Do you have family or other individuals who support your idea or venture?

How do you decide on a business?

- Research whether your previous work experience, hobbies or other interests can be turned into a business.

- Investigate how similar businesses are succeeding or not.

- Review and carefully evaluate franchise opportunities.

- Participate in both online and in-person entrepreneurial groups.

What type of compensation can you expect?

- Research what entrepreneurs for your type of business typically pay themselves.

- Be prepared to pay for business expenses before paying yourself.

Tips

✓ Research various business and franchise opportunities through legitimate and reliable sources.

✓ Talk to people who are over 60 and have started businesses or franchises about the positives and negatives. Listen carefully and be realistic about the significant work effort, time and money required for a successful business venture.

✓ Consult a financial planner and assess your situation, including the possibility of success or failure of a potential business. Do you have a backup plan?

✓ Discuss with an accountant setting up a business and how to isolate potential financial losses from your personal and retirement assets.

✓ Develop and follow a detailed business plan.

✓ Review the questions at the beginning of this section to help determine whether the risks and opportunities of becoming an entrepreneur are a good fit for you.

✓ Before making a business commitment, review and thoroughly discuss with your family and advisors.

Resources

"10 Seldom-Asked Questions to Answer Before You Buy a Franchise" *http://www.forbes.com/sites/ caroltice/2012/06/13/10-seldom-asked-questions-to-answer-before-you-buy-a-franchise/#1aaaed4e59a4* Provides some thought-provoking questions for you to answer before you consider a franchise.

"Creating a Business Plan for Your Franchise" *http://www.franchisedirect. com/information/informationforfranchisees/ creatingabusinessplanforyourfranchise/9/1455/* Discusses important elements of an effective plan.

"How to Write a Business Plan" *http://www.sba.gov/ starting-business/write-your-business-plan* Provides you with a business plan roadmap.

"Independent Business or Franchise? How to Decide" *http://www.inc.com/curtis-kroeker/independent-business-or-franchise-how-to-decide.html* Explores major differences between buying an independent business versus a franchise.

Franchise Directory *http://www.franchisegator.com/list-of-franchises* Offers a list which includes franchises, business opportunities, distributorships, licenses, and dealerships.

Entrepreneur Magazine
http://www.entrepreneur.com/magazine
Provides news stories about entrepreneurship and is
a resource for small business owners looking to open
new locations, purchase inventory or equipment, hire
new employees or fulfill other business needs.

 Franchise Opportunities *http://www.frannet.com*
Offers free consultants who provide valuable research
and guidance for buying a franchise.

 Inc. Magazine *http://www.inc.com*
Gives advice, tools and services that help small
business grow.

 Service Corps of Retired Executives (SCORE)
http://www.score.org
Helps small businesses get off the ground, grow and
achieve their goals through education and mentorship.

 Small Business Administration (SBA)
http://www.sba.gov
Offers support to entrepreneurs and small businesses.

 Starting a Business
http://www.sba.gov/starting-business
Provides numerous resources for the entrepreneur.

Notes

"You make a living by what you get.
You make a life by what you give."

—WINSTON CHURCHILL

CHAPTER 4

Volunteering—Unpaid Work

You are thinking about volunteering. You're willing and now able to make important contributions without pay. In the past, you were pressed for time between your job, family and other commitments. Now, you have some breathing room and can decide what's important to you. You're at a point in your life where you want to give back to society.

You may want to volunteer with a nonprofit that's meaningful to you based on your own experiences. Perhaps you or a family member has had a problem or an illness and you want to repay the help given or you have a commitment to a cause or belief, which you can now devote time to help with. You want the satisfaction of helping.

If you have interest in policymaking and strategy, joining a nonprofit board may be a meaningful way to serve.

You're able to donate your professional skills and possibly be willing to learn new ones.

Perhaps you want to meet new people and become involved in your community.

Volunteering keeps you busy and if the nonprofit is located close by, logistics are not a problem. As a volunteer, you'll most likely have scheduling flexibility, which can be very appealing.

There are many reasons for volunteering. Your decision to volunteer may start you on an interesting and fulfilling journey.

⇈ Advantages of volunteering:

- Studies have shown that volunteers are physically and emotionally healthier than their non-volunteering peers.

- You feel a sense of purpose and well-being by helping others.

- Your involvement makes a positive difference to the specific nonprofits and your community.

- You make new friends and by seeing people on a regular basis promote optimism.

- You'll have a flexible schedule and possibly receive invitations to events.

- You can find a variety of volunteer opportunities in your community and abroad.

⑦ If you are considering becoming a volunteer, answer these questions:

- What nonprofits interest you? Why?

- Do you understand the organization's mission?

- Do you see how you can contribute to the organization?

- Do you want to share your current skills?

- Do you want to learn something new?

- How much time can you devote to volunteering?

How do you decide where to volunteer?

You can use job-search methods to find the best volunteer fit, but most nonprofits are easily accessible and are more than willing to utilize your experience and skills.

- Determine which particular nonprofits are important to you.

- Research these targeted nonprofits for volunteer opportunities.

- Talk with friends and neighbors who are volunteering with different organizations. Ask about their experiences and recommendations.

 What type of compensation can you expect?

As a volunteer, your compensation is the satisfaction you gain by doing the meaningful work of strengthening your community by helping others.

Tips

✓ **View volunteering as an unpaid job with the same sense of commitment that you would give to a paid position.**

✓ Feel free to explore different volunteer opportunities in order to find the best fit.

✓ Try not to overextend yourself.

✓ Enjoy being a volunteer.

Resources

 American Association of Retired Persons (AARP)
http://www.aarp.org/giving-back/info-10-2012/find-volunteer-opportunities-ms1817.html
Lists local volunteer positions.

 Bridgespan Executive Search
http://www.bridgespan.org/About/Bridgestar.aspx
Offers executive search services and posts nonprofit executive level positions.

 Commongood Careers *http://commongoodcareers.org*
Provides nonprofits with innovative recruitment solutions that result in faster and better hires for paid positions.

Executive Service Corps (ESC) *http://www.escus.org*
Focuses exclusively on advising nonprofits. ESC
has worked with hundreds of nonprofits, including
schools, museums, cities, healthcare, social-service,
and other charitable organizations.

 Global Volunteers *http://globalvolunteers.org*
Assists worldwide community development programs
by mobilizing short-term volunteers on local work
programs as well as providing project funding and
child sponsorships.

 Go Abroad *http://www.goabroad.com/volunteer-abroad/
search/seniors/volunteer-abroad-1*
Posts a variety of international volunteer program
opportunities.

 Habitat for Humanity International
http://www.habitat.org/volunteer
Partners with future and current homeowners to
build simple, decent and affordable housing for low
to very low-income families. Volunteers and future
homeowners work together in the building process.

 Older Volunteers: Projects Abroad *http://www.
projects-abroad.org/how-it-works/older-volunteers*
Offers a range of meaningful short-term group trips
for established professionals and retirees over the age
of 50. Programs take place in countries across the
developing world and last over two weeks.

Openmind Projects *http://www.openmindprojects.org/retired-senior-volunteer-programs-overseas.html*
Posts volunteer opportunities in Asia.

Peace Corps *http://www.peacecorps.gov/volunteer/is-peace-corps-right-for-me/50plus*
Sends adults of all ages to work as volunteers in developing countries.

Points of Light *http://www.pointsoflight.org*
Mobilizes volunteers to take action on the causes they care about through innovative programs, events and campaigns.

RSVP *http://www.nationalservice.gov/programs/senior-corps/rsvp*
Lists community volunteer positions for people 55 and over.

Senior Corps
http://www.nationalservice.gov/programs/senior-corps
Connects people age 55 and older with service opportunities in their home communities.

Service Corps of Retire Executives (SCORE)
http://www.score.org
Helps small businesses get off the ground, grow and achieve their goals through education and mentorship. Retired business professionals serve as coaches.

United Way
http://www.unitedway.org/get-involved/volunteer
Links potential volunteers to local chapters.

Volunteer Match *http://www.volunteermatch.org*
Provides local volunteer information and listings.

Volunteers for Peace *http://vfp.org*
Offers volunteer placements in over 3,000 voluntary
service projects worldwide.

YMCA International *http://www.ymca.net*
Provides a variety of domestic volunteer programs.

Notes

_____

_____

_____

_____

_____

_____

_____

_____

_____

_____

_____

_____

_____

_____

_____

"If opportunity doesn't knock, build a door."

—MILTON BERLE

CHAPTER 5

Looking for a Job

Whether you are targeting a full-time role, part-time job, or volunteer position, the steps for success are similar.

Section 5.1 - Appearance and Personal Impact

The harsh truth is that we judge books by their covers and, in a similar fashion, you are judged by your appearance. As a Boomer, you must make the effort to project your most up-to-date appearance and energetic self. Even if you are intellectually and experience-wise able to outperform those "youngsters" in the workplace, few managers will hire you if they think you do not have a youthful attitude or if you have an outdated appearance and convey a low energy level. Fortunately, you can update your appearance and present a contemporary, industry-appropriate look as well as project vigor.

You will also be judged by your "electronic appearance." Follow these steps to make sure your communications are up-to-date:

- Make sure your email address is professional and easy to remember, preferably your first and last name (e.g. John. Doe@email provider.com).

- Review your cell phone message. A short, generic message works well.

- Buy a texting plan. Texting has become a preferred quick way of communicating.

- Research your online presence. Remember employers and recruiters check applicants' online activities for positive and negative information.

Tips

✓ Look at yourself in the mirror. How can you update your appearance? Ask a friend, spouse, close co-worker or image consultant to give you "honest" feedback.

✓ In addition to wearing stylish, appropriate apparel for your industry, remember no tight or revealing clothing. For a more refreshed look, consider coloring your hair (men and women). If you have no experience with hair coloring, go to a professional.

✓ Aging is inevitable, but doing your best to remain healthy and energetic while maintaining a youthful attitude is important to getting hired.

- Improve your physical fitness: walk, ride a bike, go to a gym.
- Whiten your teeth.
- Update your glasses.
- Get a manicure.
- For men, if you think a suit is too formal, try a sports jacket with a dress shirt and trousers or just a dress shirt and trousers.
- For women, unless you're in a creative field, tailored clothing is a good bet.
- Be cheerful and wear your biggest smile.

Resources

 "Baby Boomers: Don't Let Appearance Stand in Your Way!" *http://www.monster.ca/career-advice/article/ baby-boomers-appearance-career-tips*

 "The New Job-Interview Dress Code: For Women over 50 Competing for Employment, the Key Is to Look Current" *http://www.nextavenue.org/new-job-interview-dress-code*

 "Over-50 Job Search: Looking Young, Younger, Youngest" *http://www.job-hunt.org/boomer-job-search/ boomers-looking-younger.shtml*

Section 5.2 - Research: Industries, Companies, Contacts

Whatever work option you decide to pursue, research is an important element. You must determine what organizations interest you and how you can add value.

What do you know about your current industry or other industries you may be targeting? Perhaps you are considering a different role. Using online research and job boards is important, but take it a step further: talk to people in-person and online. Learning from others is a great way to research your market. It's also good for your sanity. You might miss the water cooler relationships and "lunch bunch" camaradie you had when you worked. We all need to interact with real people.

Identify your strengths, including both the technical skills specific to your industry and soft skills that help you work in team environments. Remember, strengths are **where what you like to do meets what you're good at.** Keep a list of those strengths. You want to be able to describe your strengths to others both verbally and in writing (e.g. "I'm organized, analytical and good at explaining technical issues to nontechnical people." Cite examples.)

Answer the following questions:

- What skills do you possess? Assess your skills realistically and be prepared to show flexibility.

- How can you help the employer? What problems can you solve? You must be able to address their specific needs with your skills.

- What value do you bring? Be able to concretely and concisely express this value (e.g. "I'm great at bringing in projects under budget and on time." Cite examples.)

While searching for your next opportunity, be open to volunteering. This activity takes you out of your house and head. Not only will you help nonprofits who never have enough staff, but you may also connect with people who either themselves can help with your job search or will refer you to someone else who can. *(See Chapter 4 for more information on volunteering.)*

Who do you know? This is the most widely missed research tool. Why? Many of us never ask for directions even when we're lost. But we would be better off if we did ask for help. We need each other. Most people that have been through a job search understand the value of networking.

Tips

- ✓ Make lists of companies you are interested in and research them via their websites. Use free information sites like Google, Yahoo Finance, Bloomberg, Hoovers, local newspapers, and the Business Journal which also includes a "Book of Lists."

- ✓ Google Maps will show you company locations in proximity to your home.

- ✓ Pretend you are a hiring authority and looking to hire someone for the specific job you want. Your company's competitors probably have similar positions. What other companies hire for your position? Prepare a list and start from there.

- ✓ Reach out. Now that you have a list of companies you are interested in, start talking to people who might be able to help you. Make a list of people you know and their potential contacts. It's a great way to find out about the market, companies and roles that you are considering.

- ✓ Ask your contacts for information about their companies, the workplace environment and industry economic outlook. They may also know about possible job openings and other connections who may be able to advance your search.

Resources

Bureau of Labor Statistics *http://www.bls.gov*
Tracks statistics on different occupations.

Glassdoor *http://www.glassdoor.com*
Provides a database of more than eight million company reviews, CEO approval ratings, salary reports, interview reviews, and questions, benefits reviews, office photos and more.

O*NET OnLine *http://www.onetonline.org*
Researches different occupations.

Vault *http://www.vault.com*
Provides employee surveys of top employers, career advice, job listings and career guides to individual industries.

Section 5.3 – Networking

Whether you are looking for paid or volunteer work, networking is essential.

You network by connecting with other people to exchange information and develop contacts especially to further your job search.

By connecting with others, you'll gain valuable information about an industry's economic outlook and specific understanding of company workplace environments as well as your potential role. Networking with people who are knowledgeable ensures that you get the right kinds of leads and support.

Networking exemplifies the Golden Rule: "Do unto others as you would have them do unto you." Just as you want assistance in finding a position, so do others. You may be able to help someone through your contacts. Becoming a resource for others is good for you and for them.

You will feel better by helping others and they'll be motivated to help you. By working the concept **"six degrees of separation"**—the idea that everyone in the world is separated from everyone else by no more than six people—you may link to someone who can help you to achieve your goals.

Making Connections

- Show your friendliness by being cheerful whether speaking on the phone, meeting someone in-person or making online contacts.

- Develop your own presentation emphasizing your experience and accomplishments.

- Through practice, become comfortable discussing your experience and how others can specifically help you.

- Although your situation is foremost in your mind, work to establish trust and become a resource for others.

- In conversations, listen and be ready to help with suggestions and share contacts you may have.

- Join appropriate professional societies and offer to help with the job bank and other activities.

- Stay in touch with new and longstanding professional contacts with appropriate emails, industry information and quick phone calls. They will remember you for referrals.

- Meet new contacts and follow up with email notes.

Tips

✓ Develop a networking plan with scheduled times for telephone calls, emails and online activities.

✓ Increase your number of potential referrals by talking to your family and friends about your plans.

✓ LISTEN to people's suggestions.

✓ Schedule "coffee" meetings with individuals to learn more about where they work and what they do.

✓ Participate in professional associations, religious groups, neighborhood meetings and fun events. The idea is to connect with people!

Resources

🖥 **Make Your Contacts Count: Networking Know-How for Business and Career Success** by Anne Baber

🖥 **Networking for People Who Hate Networking: A Field Guide for Introverts, the Overwhelmed, and the Underconnected** by Devora Zack

🖥 **The 20-Minute Networking Meeting** by Marcia Ballinger

Section 5.4 - Social Media – Networking Online

Social media has changed the way we look for work. If you aren't familiar with it, take a class or free online tutorial. You can enlist your child, grandchild or neighbor for social media lessons. YouTube has extensive online tutorials.

In-house recruiters, human resources professionals, talent managers and search firms all rely heavily on social media to find candidates. LinkedIn is a free venue which enables you to showcase your skills and strengths in a profile. You'll become visible in this professional community and able to connect with people who can potentially help you.

Create a LinkedIn profile that reflects your important skills. As with your resume, list information that describes your last 15 years, no more. Connect with former co-workers, friends and people with whom you did business. Expand your network by connecting with decision makers, recruiters and people at your target organizations or in a field you want to be in.

LinkedIn today is used by 90 percent of recruiters to source candidates. Even if you don't use social media regularly, at the minimum develop a LinkedIn profile, so you can be seen and possibly discovered.

Spend time to stay engaged with this LinkedIn community in the following ways:

- Post weekly at least one-to-two status updates. These can include interesting articles or specific industry information.

- Start or comment on various discussion threads each week. You must become a member of a group in order to participate.

- Reach out to people who view your profile. The more you post, the more people will notice and respond to you.

The information you provide to others will make you appreciated as a resource and those you help will remember you when opportunities arise.

Tips

- ✓ Become proficient in maneuvering through social media by accessing free online tutorials, attending a course or seeking help from a friend.

- ✓ Develop a strong Linkedin profile by using Linkedin, YouTube and other helpful online tutorials.

- ✓ Explore Facebook including the business page option.

- ✓ Connect with friends, former colleagues and people you know professionally. Remember: they and their networks may help you.

Resources

 Facebook *http://www.facebook.com*
Connects you with working professionals, from business owners to professionals who may be involved in hiring.

 LinkedIn *http://www.linkedin.com*
Provides valuable recruitment and hiring tool for employers. You can network with other professionals in your industry and apply to job postings.

 Meetup *http://www.meetup.com*
Forms groups based on peoples' specific interests, including job search.

 Twitter *http://twitter.com*
Sends short text messages ("tweets") of up to 140 characters long. Joining will increase your exposure to a large network of people in various fields as well as companies and hiring managers who are increasingly sharing open positions.

YouTube *http://www.youtube.com/*
Offers videos on a variety of topics, including social media.

Section 5.5 - Writing a Resume

A resume is your marketing brochure, emphasizing who you are and what you can do for your future employer. Whether you are considering a full-time, consulting or part-time job, a resume is essential. Even a volunteer position may require a resume or a letter of interest. *(See Appendices for examples.)*

Keep your resume to two pages, maximum. Potential employers will not read a longer version unless you are applying to an academic or a scientific field that involves patents, publishing and research.

Key words are IMPORTANT! They will help you maneuver through electronic filters called Applicant Tracking Systems (ATS) which most companies use to "view" and eliminate resumes that do not seem to be a good fit. These systems compare the key words in your resume to the position description.

If a particular job is a good fit for your experience, tailor your resume specifically, using the corresponding job description keywords. *(See the Appendices for Sample Resumes.)*

For practice with finding the "right" key words for your resume, try this exercise. Find six great job descriptions. Copy and paste all of them into one document. Go to *http://www.tagcrowd.com* and paste the document into the box. You will get a word cloud in which the words among the six job descriptions that show up most often are displayed in larger print than the others. These will be the key words that should be in your reume.

Generally, employers are interested in your more recent experience. Deemphasize your age by removing the dates from your education and limit your work experience to the last 10-15 years, which will help keep your resume to two pages.

Tips

✓ Write your resume in a simple and easy-to-read format—no personal pronouns.

✓ Triple-check for typos and grammar and spelling errors.

✓ Use word processing software like MS Word which has several templates to help create your resume. Ask people in your network to review your resume and provide feedback.

✓ Tailor your resume to the specific job description.

Resources

 American Association of Retired Persons (AARP)
*http://www.aarp.org/work/job-hunting/info-07-2008/
writing_winning_resume.html*
A nonprofit organization that provides a variety of
information for seniors, including resume examples.

 Word Cloud site *http://www.tagcrowd.com*
A web application for visualizing word frequencies
in any text by creating what is popularly known as a
word cloud, text cloud or tag cloud.

Notes

_____

_____

_____

_____

_____

_____

_____

_____

_____

_____

_____

_____

_____

_____

_____

_____

"I'm a great believer in luck, and I find the harder I work, the more I have of it."

—THOMAS JEFFERSON

CHAPTER 6

Interviewing

Interviews have changed significantly in the last 10 years. More than likely, you will be interviewed by someone younger than you. You must engage with this person and relate your positive work experiences to this younger generation.

Emphasize that you are physically active and therefore are able to keep up with the rest of the workforce. Activities such as swimming, tennis, racquetball and running as well as going to the gym, suggest that you are fit and can manage the workload.

It's important that you do not exhibit the stereotype of an older worker having little energy, not being familiar with technology or unable to work with younger colleagues.

Age discrimination is alive and well. If you speak too pensively and often pause, you may be perceived as old and slow. Perceptions are reality to the interviewer. Bring an electronic tablet to the interview for note-taking rather than writing on paper.

Boomers perpetuate negative stereotypes by such comments as, "I'm having a senior moment." If you can do the work and want the job, then forever remove such phrases from your vocabulary.

Section 6.1 Phone Interviews

In the past, phone interviews were conducted by Human Resources personnel primarily to gather work history details and to gauge any obvious problems such as poor language skills. With the large number of applicants per position, employers today are actually using the phone interview as a real interview rather than a pre-interview. By doing this they can eliminate the majority of applicants and offer in-person interviews to a targeted few.

How should I prepare for a phone screen?

- Do your best to schedule your phone call when you have access to a phone with good reception, no interruptions and quiet space. No dogs barking in the background.

- Use an animated tone of voice and stand up while interviewing to project your energy and enthusiasm.

- If you have the interviewers' names, look them up on LinkedIn and in a search engine such as Google.

- Do not ask about compensation. Wait for the interviewer to bring up this subject.

- Have your resume, job description and a "cheat sheet" with reminders in front of you.

- The cheat sheet should include the following:
  - Specific experience related to the job requirements.
  - Your unique selling points which are applicable to this job.
  - Job history issues on resume, such as reasons for job changes, long unemployment periods, etc.
  - Facts about the company you're interviewing with.
  - Your weaknesses, such as projects that didn't go well and what positive lessons you learned.
  - Your strengths. Be ready to speak about your accomplishments and positive experiences working with younger employees.
  - If applicable, discuss your software and social media knowledge.

- Your last job's compensation or your current compensation expectations. Be familiar with your total compensation, which includes base salary, bonus, profit sharing, vacation, holidays, healthcare and other insurances, employee assistance programs, dependent care, education, and other reimbursements.

• Be prepared to answer the question, "Why do you want to work here and why should we hire you?"

Section 6.2 - Video Interviews

Online video job interviews are increasing in popularity.

Recruiters and hiring managers regularly conduct real-time video interviews that take place remotely, using applications such as Skype or FaceTime. The hiring manager poses questions to the applicant, who responds in real-time. Video job interviews can replace the initial in-person screenings. This method eases scheduling issues and eliminates costly travel for both employer and applicant.

Recruiters and hiring managers also use asynchronous job video interviews when real-time interviewing isn't needed. The recruiter or hiring manager provides questions for the specific job. Applicants receive a web link which connects them to the site where they have a specified amount of time to answer each question. These interviews can be undertaken at the applicant's convenience. The video recording is sent to the hiring manager and distributed to others involved in hiring.

We will concentrate on the real-time interview. With proper preparation you can impress your interviewer and gain the opportunity to meet face-to-face.

Prior to the actual interview, you can rehearse interviewing with a friend, using a real-time video application. *(See Section 6.4 for sample interview questions.)* Your friend can tell you if the technical quality of the sound and visuals needs to be adjusted. Try to record the interview, so you can assess and improve your presentation. By rehearsing, you will become comfortable with video interviewing.

How should you prepare for a video interview?

- The interviews are prescheduled and you will be told which software to use and details on how to connect.

- Decide whether you are going to use a desktop computer, notebook or tablet for the interview.

- Test your downloaded software before the interview.

- Contact your interviewer if you have technical problems.

- Dress professionally.

- Select a quiet, neat, uncluttered room with a table or desk. The background should be neutral with no visual distractions.

- Prepare neat notes for your interview. You have done your company and interviewer research. Place your resume and cheat sheet in front of you. *(See Section 6.1 for more information about interview preparation.)*

- Sit comfortably with good posture at a clean table that holds your notes.

- Position the webcam, so that you are framed from the waist up, not just your face is visible.

- Look at the camera, not at your computer screen.

- Be attentive, lean in a bit. Do not speak over the interviewer.

- Limit your hand movements, so you appear calm.

- Show your natural friendliness, smile.

Section 6.3 - In-Person Interviews

You have passed the first screenings and have secured an in-person interview.

Most interviewers follow behavior-based interviewing techniques. The belief here is that past work behavior is a strong indicator of future behavior and performance. You'll be asked to give specific examples of work situations that show how you did your job and be expected to explain the specific situation, the action you took and the results.

Along with your updated appearance, you must convey exuberance and bounce. From the moment you enter a room, whether it's a restaurant or a reception area, you are being evaluated.

Think 45—carry yourself with your 45-year-old spark!
Make sure you have eaten before your interview. If you
drink caffeine, have a beverage before your job interview.
You want to project energy!

Human Resources in-house recruiters, agency recruiters
and actual hiring authorities are interested in hiring the
best candidate for the position. These professionals are
not your buddies, so do not confide in them. They have a
mission to complete the search quickly, so they can move
on to the next project.

Show that you are the best candidate by clearly
communicating your energy, attitude and specific
expertise as well as the fact that you fit into their company
environment—which you can learn about through
networking and online research.

Some other advice to consider:

- One of the definitions for "Game Face" is looking and
  hopefully feeling confident when you are about to tackle
  something difficult or when you are about to take on
  a challenge. So put on your Game Face and give the
  hiring authority strong reasons why you should be
  hired.

- Try to establish a bond between you and your
  interviewer by finding something you have in common.
  If you cannot find such information, look at his/her
  desk, ask questions or comment about casual interests.

Being able to develop a friendly chemistry with the interviewer will start your interview off on a positive note.

- Stay cheerful and professional.

- Prepare a personal narrative that leads to your professional story. Where are you from? How did you decide to go into this field? Always include humor. Then practice your story at least 30 times until it becomes a natural part of your networking and interviewing repertoire which can be tweaked as needed.

Example: *I'm from Michigan and a Texan by choice. I'm the middle child of three and have always negotiated my way between the first born and the baby. I've had to be the flexible one. I'm also the first college graduate in my family. I've always been good with numbers, so becoming an accountant and later a CPA was a good choice for me. I like the challenge of making everything balance. I worked part-time in order to go to college and by necessity have had to multi-task and manage my time well. What else would you like to know?*

How should you prepare for an in-person interview?

- Energetically "bounce" into the interview and maintain high energy until you have left the building.

- Feel confident. You look up-to-date and have the right experience.

- Do not give off an attitude of entitlement.

- Bring two to four copies of your resume.

- Sit up straight with confident posture. Keep friendly eye contact and SMILE.

- Have your narrative polished, ready and appropriate for the position.

- Speak clearly and share your specific, positive experiences about working with younger employees.

- Come prepared with questions about the company's current and possible future role in its industry.

- Do not ask about benefits or compensation. The employer or recruiter will bring up this discussion.

- Let the interviewer know your interest before you leave. "I want this position. What are your next steps in the hiring process?" Be sure to communicate your enthusiasm and readiness to start work.

Tips

- ✓ If you feel you have trouble being easily understood, consider specific training to modify your speech or accent.

- ✓ Make sure, your interview clothing fits well and looks good, days before the actual interview.

- ✓ Practice responses to interview questions with a friend or former colleague.

- ✓ Call your cell phone and leave your presentation. Call back and listen. Are you loud enough? Do you have energy in your voice? Is your presentation too long? Re-record and get your introduction pared down to 35-60 seconds.

- ✓ When you have an in-person interview, check the driving and parking situation or bus schedule route before the day. Plan to arrive fifteen minutes early.

- ✓ Eat before the interview, so you feel energized.

Resources

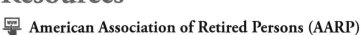

American Association of Retired Persons (AARP)
http://search.aarp.org/gss/everywhere?q=job%20 interview&intcmp=DSO-SRCH-EWHERE
Lists many job search resources including interviewing.

American Speech Hearing Language Society
http://www.asha.org/public/speech/development/accent-modification
Provides a national directory of speech pathologists who offer speech modification training.

Monster.com *http://www.monster.com/career-advice/ article/job-search-resources-older-workers*
Offers job search advice, articles and job listings.

Quintessential LiveCareer *http://www.livecareer.com/ quintessential/sample-behavioral*
Provides a variety of job search materials and advice.

YouTube *http://www.youtube.com/results?search_ query=video+job+interviews*
Offers numerous helpful videos on different types of interviewing and job search.

Section 6.4 - Sample Interview Questions

Remember you are over 60 and more than likely the interviewer is much younger than you. You must show that you like and can keep up with the "youngsters." Generic responses have little value. All interviewers seek specific answers to questions.

Here are some sample interview questions:

1. Tell me about yourself.

Your objective: Establish rapport with interviewer and present yourself in a competent, appealing way. Start with a friendly narrative.

Example: *I always wanted to be a pilot but there were so few job opportunities that I became more realistic and discovered a talent for numbers. I excelled in my accounting classes. I love my field and have always enjoyed its challenges. I like working on the details as well as understanding the big picture.*

2. You've been unemployed for a long time, why?

Your objective: To show that you are looking for a good fit and that you've maintained and updated your skills.

Examples: *I don't want just any job. I want to find a good fit where I can do my best work. My company eliminated my department, so I've been keeping up to date in my field by staying active in my professional society and taking _____ courses. I've taken this time to explore other ventures. I've done a bit of consulting (be prepared to provide*

details about this consulting) and have realized that I enjoy
being part of a team rather than going solo.

3. What position are you looking for?

Your objective: You are looking for the position for which
you are interviewing. Show your familiarity with this
position and explain why you are a great fit.

Example: *This position is a great fit for me based on*
my experience and interests. I have the enthusiasm and
_____ experience to do a super job.

4. Tell me specifically how your experience relates to this position.

Your objective: Match your experience to the specifics of
the position.

Example: *I'm experienced in all areas of regulatory reporting,*
including U.S. GAAP accounting and SEC reporting
standards.

5. What do you know about our company?

Your objective: To show your serious interest in this
position by being very knowledgeable about the company.
Research the company using various online resources
for information on the history, company milestones and
current situation.

Example: *Well, your company was started in Oklahoma by*
the _____family, manufacturing _____
products. Today you've diversified from this small enterprise

into an international corporation with multiple businesses. Your market share is _____. I'm quite impressed.

6. We have a diverse work force. Give me examples of your experience working with younger employees.

Your objective: Show your respect and ability to work effectively with younger workers.

Example: *Diversity is the strength of any workplace. I've enjoyed working with younger employees. We can learn from each other. I've always collaborated with whoever was on the team. I respect their opinions whether as my manager or co-worker. I believe that by working together we'll come up with the best solutions. I worked with the I.T. department to develop a manual that nontechies could understand. Everyone in the IT department was significantly younger than me and many were from different countries. We worked well together.*

7. You seem overqualified for this position.

Your objective: Prove you will not leave this company for a better position or retire in the near future.

Example: *I have reached the point in my career where I want to concentrate on work that I enjoy and do well. Titles are not important. I plan to continue working for a long time and gain the satisfaction of being able to contribute to your company.*

8. We pride ourselves on our company's use of the latest technology. Describe your technology expertise.

Your objective: Show that you are up-to-date and continue to learn.

Example: *Of course, in my previous position, I used _____, _____ and _____ programs. I'm always eager to learn new applications. I'm currently taking an online course in _____.*

9. Tell me about a time when you were not successful. What happened and what did you take away from this experience?

Your objective: Relate a specific situation and the lesson learned.

Example: *I was working on the company newsletter, which included employee-written articles. I assumed that these highly educated employees were good writers, so I included their articles 'as is'. Huge mistake—their articles needed editing. I learned from this experience to never assume anything and after that, I reviewed and edited all newsletter submissions.*

10. What inspires you in a job?

Your objective: Show your work ethic and comprehensive view of this position.

Example: *I like challenges and the feeling of accomplishment. Tough deadlines get my adrenaline flowing and I do whatever it takes to complete the assignment.*
I worked on completing an assessment of HR Software

systems. Well, we were already close to our end of financial year deadline when a new vendor's product was added to the list to be reviewed. This purchase order had to be submitted before the budget year ended. I worked nonstop to complete my appraisal of the systems and made my recommendation. The purchase order was processed in time.

11. How do you keep up to date in your field?

Your objective: Show specific actions toward increasing and maintaining knowledge.

Example: *I subscribe to online publications and participate in my professional society as well as have recently completed _____ courses.*

12. Are you an optimist or pessimist?

Your objective: Show your friendly, positive, upbeat view of life.

Example: *I'm optimistic with a sense of reality. I try to plan, so a good outcome is possible. Our department reported to a new VP. Everyone was quite worried. I managed to persuade them that just doing our best work possible was the way to show our value to the new boss. I was right. The new VP commended my department on its great performance.*

13. What are your weaknesses?

Your objective: Show weaknesses that were neutralized or turned into strengths.

Example: *I have a tendency to believe my project is absolutely vital, however, I've learned that everyone else has equally important work and if I expect help with mine, I must be available to them. I needed to get several peoples' sign-off on a particular project and told myself that they too had deadlines, so I worked around their schedules. They ultimately helped me and later I was able to reciprocate.*

14. If we talked to your boss, what would she say about you?

Your objective: Reveal positive attributes with minor negatives.

Example: *She would say, I'm the go-to-person for my department and can be counted on to get projects done under tight deadlines. She would also say that I need to work on tempering my intensity and not be so driven. In other words, relax more.*

15. Give me an example of a time you had to deal with a difficult person and the result?

Your objective: Every company has difficult clients. Demonstrate how you successfully handled such a situation.

Example: *Well, my colleagues tell me I'm really good at working with difficult customers. We had a gentleman who* *was very upset about his account statement. I was able to patiently explain all the charges on the statement. He left as a satisfied customer.*

16. What are your strengths?

Your objective: Show strengths relevant to this position.

Example: *I am a big-picture person with the patience and aptitude for detailed work. I led a team and explained the scope and vision for the project. When two members were out sick and my deadline was fast approaching, I quickly took over their responsibilities to complete the work on time.*

17. Where do you see yourself in a couple of years?

Your objective: Show you are planning to stay with company for a while and not retire or leave for a better offer.

Example: *I plan to stay and do the best job I can for you. I'm happy with wherever my good work takes me in this company.*

18. This is a part-time job with a different schedule each week. We need a dependable person who can finish the receivables in the time allotted.

Your objective: This is your opportunity to show what value you bring to the job.

Examples: *I had been a volunteer in a nonprofit's accounting department for the last four years. There I worked three mornings a week and definitely got my work done in a short* *period of time. I'm flexible and a part-time position is exactly what I want.*

19. What is least appealing to you about this part-time job?

Your objective: Every job has a boring element, show the interviewer you understand the importance of the task and can do the work with good cheer.

Example: *Filing patient records can be a bit tedious, but I realize the importance of easily accessible patient records in a doctor's office. In previous jobs, I've always been complimented on my attention to detail, dependability and friendly attitude. I would also enjoy welcoming and scheduling patients as well as doing whatever else needs to be done.*

20. You've held high-powered positions, why would you want this part-time position?

Your objective: Explain why you are going from a leadership position to an individual contributor role or from a full-time position to part-time one.

Example: *At this point in my career, I want less stress and more time to do the kind of work I enjoy. This part-time role is perfect because it would allow me to use my experience to do a great job and also give me time for my hobbies.*

21. How do you measure success?

Your objective: Your response will give the interviewer insight as to your values, work ethic and goals.

Example: *On one level, success for me, means accomplishing my daily work goals and possibly solving a demanding problem. But equally important is doing my best to help my customers and co-workers. I want to feel a sense of accomplishment about my day's work.*

22. What are your hobbies?

Your objective: Show you are energetic and able to keep up with younger employees.

Example: *I'm a Scout leader and spend a lot of time outdoors hiking with my troop.*

23. What are your salary requirements?

Your objective: Show you care about this position, want to be paid the market rate and have confidence in the employer.

Example: *What is your range or budget for this job? I want this position and am certain that we can agree on equitable compensation.*

24. Why should we hire you?

Your objective: Show your desire and experience are a great fit for this position.

Example: *My work is important to me. I want and understand this job. I'm enthusiastic and committed to doing the best work possible. Based on my experience and commitment, I will become a productive member of your team.*

25. Do you have questions for us?

Your objective: Learn the interviewer's perception of you and time frame for decision-making process. You can provide the details to alleviate the interviewer's concerns.

Example: *Are there any areas in my experience that you feel hesitant about? I can understand why you wonder if I have enough experience in _____. Although my resume doesn't go into detail about_____. I worked for __years in _____and _____.*

Section 6.5 - Interview Follow-up

In today's world, many job seekers forgo follow-up. Show that you're different by sending a written or email thank you for the opportunity to interview. *(See Appendices for a sample thank you note.)* Good follow-up is an indicator of the type of employee you will be. You can ensure strong follow-up to your interview by doing the following:

- Get a business card from everyone you meet.

- Send an email emphasizing your fit for the position and eagerness to come on board.

- Do not send the same follow-up note to multiple interviewers.

- After you send a thank you note, follow up with another email (within the time frame the interviewer said the hiring decision would be made) and reiterate your interest.

Section 6.6 - Background Checks and References

Employers and volunteer organizations increasingly require background as well as credit checks and references. Review your resume for accuracy and answer background and credit questions truthfully.

Provide your references with the details for each position for which you are applying and ask them for their support. If they seem reluctant, find other references.

Notes

"You'll never please everyone, but you only have to please a few people to get an offer."

—HARVEY MACKAY

CHAPTER 7

Negotiating Offers

Section 7.1 - Negotiation Strategies

Know your market value. Do some research on salary sites to understand the compensation range for the position, industry, company size and your level of experience. Remember, even if you are unemployed, it's okay to ask for compensation based on your research and specific experience. The company may not meet it, but offers are rarely rescinded because you negotiate. Although some companies negotiate the compensation package prior to giving a final offer, most will give you an offer with room for later negotiation. Keep in mind:

- You do not have an offer until you have received one in writing. Most companies make offers once they are reasonably certain that the applicant is truly interested in the position, not job shopping.

- Since you have the offer in writing, you know the company believes you are the best person for the job and therefore have room to negotiate. Take into consideration the job market and your personal situation.

- The negotiation process is not an adversarial one. Both you and the company want a positive outcome.

- Once you receive a written job offer, tell the employer you will review it and respond. Employers don't expect you to respond without evaluating the offer first.

- If the offer is not all that you want, decide on your absolute deal-breakers and the giveaways that are not as important to you.

- Your attitude, much like the one you had during the interview, must be positive and upbeat. Cheerfully ask questions and do not make demands. Give specific, realistic justifications for increasing the compensation.

Examples of how to open compensation negotiations:

You must open negotiations in a way that makes you comfortable and is suitable for the industry in which you'll be working. Note the difference in tone between the following two openings:

I'm interested in this position, but feel we need to discuss the compensation package further. Let's set up a time for discussion.

OR

Thank you for this opportunity. I'm excited about this position and want to become a contributing member of your team. After reviewing the offer, I would like to discuss some points a bit more with you. When can we set up a time to talk?

Before you discuss compensation with the employer:

- Be prepared with relevant information to make your case.

- Have realistic expectations if you are changing fields or industries or are moving from a large company to a small one.

- Assess your personal situation. Are you employed and searching for a better position or currently unemployed?

- Write two counter proposals to the offer for yourself. By putting your concerns in writing you will focus on important issues and not get sidetracked.

- The first counter proposal should include increased base salary with specific justification and any other issues that need to be addressed.

- The second counter proposal should assume that the salary is nonnegotiable and define other benefits that are important to you such as a signing bonus, more vacation days, flex time, etc.

- Once the negotiations are completed, you cannot go back and try to renegotiate. If you try to do this, the company may withdraw the offer.

- If the negotiation goes well and you are satisfied with the results, smile and join the new company.

Section 7.2 - What to do if the offer after negotiation is not satisfactory?

You must seriously evaluate your own situation. Here are some questions to consider:

- Is this opportunity worthwhile to you?

- Can you do good work for this company at this compensation?

- Can you develop experience within this company that will stimulate a better internal position or, if need be, better outside job offers?

These are difficult questions to answer but essential to your decision-making.

If you decide not to take the position, decline the offer in a pleasant and professional manner—don't burn bridges. Your job search continues but remember that if one employer saw your value, so will others.

Tips

✓ Research your value in the market using salary surveys.

✓ Evaluate your job search and financial situation.

✓ Reflect on what's more important to you in terms of negotiable items: maybe increased vacation days makes up for a nonnegotiable salary, etc.

Resources

Payscale *(http://www.payscale.com)*
Gives free information on a variety of salary concerns.

Salary.com *(http://salary.com)*
Provides a free salary calculator to determine "What's my worth?" and other compensation data.

Salary Expert *(https://www.salaryexpert.com)*
Offers free salary, cost of living and benefits information.

Section 7.3 - Going Forward: Be a Resource for Others

You've hopefully achieved your goal of a paid or volunteer work position. You have options, unlike the previous generations who reached their 60s and were expected to retire. Boomers have changed the workplace landscape.

Perhaps your job search was a challenging quest. You refined your resume and presentation. You impressed your interviewers as the best candidate with your experience, energy and ability to work with younger employees. Yes, you're older, but you retain your youthful fire and flexibility. You are relieved or thrilled to have achieved your goal. Your work might be all-consuming or not. You feel more confident and know it is possible to find work even when you are no longer a youngster. You also have the tools to look for that next opportunity. You have every right to feel good about your accomplishment but also think about other Boomers who need help.

Remember your own experience and become a resource for others in your former situation. Be generous with your time and offer advice and referrals. You can now guide and inspire other Boomers. You are proof that Boomers provide the spark and talent essential to continuing to make a positive difference in the paid work and volunteer world.

Notes

_____

_____

_____

_____

_____

_____

_____

_____

_____

_____

_____

_____

_____

_____

_____

_____

_____

Note on the Appendices

The **bold** keywords in the Appendices Job Descriptions and similar **bold** keywords in the resumes are meant for instructional purposes only.

Do not bold keywords in your own resumes.

Most profiles are followed by job descriptions and corresponding resumes.

Resume keywords related to job description requirements are **bold** in both documents.

APPENDIX A: RESUME

NAME

City, State, Zip Code
_____

Phone Number   email address   LinkedIn URL

POSITION TITLE

Describe here who you are professionally (e.g. "accountant") and describe what value you bring, your strengths and skills. Use present tense, no personal pronouns, no complete sentences. Core competencies include the important keywords listed in the job description.

- First key word or phrase
- Second key word or phrase
- Third key word or phrase

SKILLS

- _____
- _____
- _____

- _____
- _____
- _____

- _____
- _____
- _____

PROFESSIONAL EXPERIENCE

Only include the last 10-15 years of your experience, no months listed.
COMPANY NAME, City, State   **20XX – 20XX**
Job Title
Work Responsibilities Summary condensed to two to four sentences.

- Write accomplishments, using active strong, past tense verbs. **With key words, emphasize experience that relates to job description**. Show results and use metrics where possible. **Add one accomplishment per year for each position.**
- Accomplishment #1
- Accomplishment #2
- Accomplishment #3

COMPANY NAME, City, State   **20XX – 20XX**
Job Title
Work Responsibilities Summary condensed to two to four sentences.

- Write accomplishments, using active strong, past tense verbs. **With keywords, emphasize experience that relates to job description.** Show results and use metrics where possible. Add one accomplishment per year for each position.
- Accomplishment #1
- Accomplishment #2
- Accomplishment #3

COMPANY NAME, City, State   **20XX – 20XX**
Job Title
Work Responsibilities Summary condensed to two to four sentences.
- Write accomplishments, using active strong, past tense verbs. **With keywords, emphasize experience that relates to job description.** Show results that use metrics where possible. Add one accomplishment per year for each position.
- Accomplishment #1
- Accomplishment #2
- Accomplishment #3

COMPANY NAME, City, State   **20XX – 20XX**
Job Title
Work Responsibilities Summary condensed to two to four sentences.
- Write accomplishments, using active strong, past tense verbs. **With keywords, emphasize experience that relates to job description.** Show results that use metrics where possible. Add one accomplishment per year for each position.
- Accomplishment #1
- Accomplishment #2
- Accomplishment #3

ADDITIONAL EXPERIENCE

If you want to show work experience older than 15 years, list the company name, job title with no employment dates.

COMPANY NAME, City, State
Job Title

COMPANY NAME, City, State
Job Title

EDUCATION / LICENSURE

MS, _____, University Name, City, State
BS, _____ University Name, City, State
Licenses/Certifications, Organization, City, State
Professional Societies (list)
Software Proficiencies (list)

APPENDIX B: COVER LETTER

Date

Company Name
Address

RE: Position Name / Posting #

Dear **[Name of contact],**
If you cannot find the name of the recruiter/HR contact /hiring manager,
you could use their generic title "Hiring Manager" or leave off the salutation.

Your posting for **[Name of position]** on **[Location where you saw the job**
posting] attracted my attention. For your convenience, I have listed how my
experience and strengths match the requirements of this position.
- **List first requirement from original job posting (e.g. "Must have PE with**
  engineering experience in mechanical design").

I am an experienced Mechanical Design Engineer PE with a background in
new product design and production. My experience includes hydraulic and
electromechanical systems design.
- **List second requirement from original job posting (e.g. "Experience**
  required in industrial product development from design through
  development"). Briefly note your qualification. Be sure it is reflected on
  your resume.

I have over 10 years industrial experience working from product design through
production. In addition I have supervised and trained technicians. I also
documented all processes which led to a successful ISO certification.

There are other areas in my background that could benefit **[Company name]**. I
look forward to discussing how I can assist you in meeting your goals.

I will call you next week to arrange a time for this conversation.
If you do not know the name of the hiring manager or recruiter, omit the
above sentence.

Sincerely,
Name
Email Address
Cell Phone

100

APPENDIX C: THANK YOU NOTE

Dear [**Ms. or Mr. Contact's last name**],

Thank you for the opportunity to interview for **(Name of position)**. It was great to meet with you and I am very excited about the possibility of joining your team.

You mentioned that the top priorities for this position will be **(List the top two-three requirements from the interview)** and **(List other important interview highlights.)**

I have a strong background in both areas and believe my proven skills, combined with my experience in **(Cite relevant experiences)**, would be a good fit.

I have worked on **(Cite past work/volunteer/project experiences.)**

I am a team player who enjoys a challenge and am eager to become a contributing member of your organization.

Please let me know if you need any additional information.

I appreciate your consideration and look forward to speaking with you soon.

Sincerely,
Name
Email Address
Cell Phone

APPENDIX D: PROFILES OF SUCCESSFUL WORK SEEKERS

Minister, Religious Calling

Jim, 61, had been a software developer/project manager with several companies. He had liked his work, but felt compelled to try something different and responded to a ministry call. Jim had been active in his church community and liked the idea of serving a congregation. After much prayer, he decided to pursue training for the ministry. Today Jim is a minister and very happy that he pursued his calling.

Entrepreneur, Pizza Franchise

Bob, 68, was a marketing director with a consumer goods company. He retired, but wanted to stay active and was financially well off. Bob was very close with his adult children and wanted to help his sons start a business. Together they bought a pizza franchise. Bob and his sons divided the responsibilities and are growing the business to include additional sites. He finds satisfaction in returning to work, but this time is establishing a family business for himself and his children.

Volunteer, Adult Literacy Tutor

Jane, 64, worked in outside sales for most of her career. Once she retired, Jane was ready to visit her grandchildren, travel and volunteer. She had always been civic-minded and supported many philanthropic causes. Jane needed a volunteer option which allowed her to do something meaningful and still have flexibility for family and travel. She was familiar with various volunteer opportunities and decided to become an adult-literacy volunteer. Jane schedules her trips to coincide with the nonprofit's calendar. She feels her life has great balance by being able to devote her energies to philanthropic activities as well as family time and travel.

(See Exhibits D.1, D.2, D.3, D.4, D.5 and D.6 for additional profiles, position descriptions and resumes.)

EXHIBIT D.1

Mechanical Engineer

Tom, 60, a mechanical engineer, worked in manufacturing. With his very specific technical experience, he had managed to avoid being laid off through several rounds. Even though Tom knew his luck would end, he was shocked to get his notice. His wife worked, but they were a two-income family with three children, twins in college and one child in high school. Tom started his job search and became active in his professional society. He polished his networking skills. After several months of constant networking, he landed a position with an engineering staffing company. Tom is updating his skills because he knows job security does not exist.

Position Description

Job Title: Manufacturing Design Engineer #1608B

ATech Staffing Company has been in business for over 30 years and excels at meeting our industrial clients' specific professional staffing requirements. We have long-term contracts for engineers to work at our industrial manufacturing clients' locations.

Description:

Manufacturing Design Engineer with prototype engineering experience will develop new product/process designs and support existing ones in the construction equipment segment. Goals include decreasing production time by streamlining processes which result in cost savings.

Responsibilities:

- Provide design and manufacturing support of hydraulic and electromechanical systems for existing and new product design.
- Act as liaison between internal operations and external customer regarding product design and needs.
- Develop designs to meet customer's requirements using 3-D Modeling and AutoCAD.
- Work with procurement and production to prototype customer's design.
- Trouble shoot manufacturing problems related to process and product design issues.
- Maintain document control system for entire process from design to production.
- Support ISO certification.
- Streamline processes to decrease production time and costs.
- Supervise and train technicians.

Requirements:

- BS Mechanical Engineering—advanced degree preferred.
- P.E. License.
- Strong manufacturing environment experience.
- 3-D modeling, AutoCAD and CNC Programming experience.
- ISO 9000 certification experience.
- Supervisory experience.
- Customer service experience.
- Excellent verbal and writing skills.

Benefits:

- Competitive hourly rate
- Contractor benefits
- Exposure to top manufacturing firms

Please submit your resume to www.AtechStaffing.com

TOM, P.E.

City, State, Zip Code

Cell   email address   LinkedIn URL

MANUFACTURING DESIGN ENGINEER

Mechanical Engineer with strong manufacturing track record of driving production efforts for existing and new products. Skilled in prototype engineering to complete industrial product design as well as testing of hydraulic and electro-mechanical systems design. Practiced in providing quality customer service. Experienced supervisor and trainer. Able communicator with excellent verbal and writing skills.

EXPERTISE

- Design Engineering
- Product Development
- Design Analysis
- Employee Training
- Document Management
- Regulatory Compliance
- ISO 9000
- Project Management
- Customer Service

TECHNICAL SKILLS

- 3-D Modeling / AutoCAD
- Hydraulic System Design
- Industrial Vehicle Design
- Prototype Engineering
- ASME Codes & Standards
- Electro-Mechanical Design
- CNC Programming
- Troubleshooting
- Acceptance Testing

PROFESSIONAL EXPERIENCE

COMPANY NAME, City, State   20XX – 20XX

Mechanical Design Engineer

Designed manufacturing components for construction equipment. Explained design analysis and relayed changes in drawings to design team. Supervised five staff engineers during resolution of production issues.

- Led inaugural production run of equipment, resulting in production of fifty units on schedule.
  - Trained technicians in proper assembly procedures
  - Managed delivery and inspection of part kits
  - Monitored technicians for time studies to control costs
  - Streamlined processes and distribution of tasks between technicians
- Produced largest single day equipment delivery in company history by managing production of equipment modification kits for forty units, including hiring, training and supervising ten production technicians, providing technical support to technicians and performing quality commissioning of completed units.

TOM, P.E.   **PAGE TWO**

- During highest production quarter, researched and gathered specifications for critical unit parts from suppliers; ensured parts available for immediate production. Documented all production/engineering processes; led to successful ISO certification.

COMPANY NAME, City, State   **20XX – 20XX**
Manufacturing Engineer
Developed in-house tooling for production parts per ISO 9001 quality standards. Built CAD models from customer requests. Produced drawings for manufacture of components from customer specifications. Created drawings for outsource production tasks. Developed streamlined procedures which resulted in cost savings.
- Created 3-D model of parts (from customer specifications) to be manufactured, produced rapid-prototype template parts; resulted in 30% decrease in tooling shop production and successful completion of sixty parts within six-month deadline.
- Implemented process to produce rapid prototype parts for new venture into additional market; resulted in two-day decrease in shop production time and increased ability to produce complex tooling.

COMPANY NAME, City, State   **20XX – 20XX**
Design Engineer
Designed and fabricated prototype projects. Provided technical support and documentation for production and customer service for day-to-day operations.
- Designed, built and tested prototype models for compliance with new regulations. Compliance allowed for continued sales of units.
- Designed and developed new electronic control package to upgrade machines, resulting in increased machine reliability and 10% cost savings. Conducted consumer testing, ensuring design met customer needs. Reviewed customer feedback for future improvements.

ADDITIONAL RELEVANT EXPERIENCE

COMPANY NAME, City, State
Senior Project Engineer

EDUCATION / LICENSURE

MS, Mechanical Engineering, University, City, State
BS, Mechanical Engineering, University, City, State
PE License, #123456789, State, USA

EXHIBIT D.2

Second Career, Real Estate Professional

Carol, 63, was a single mom who raised her children on an elementary school teacher's salary. When she retired, she joined book clubs, worked out at the gym and occasionally traveled. Even with all those activities, Carol felt lonely and dissatisfied. Her best friend sold real estate and encouraged her to consider the field as a career possibility. Carol did her due diligence and decided that real estate was interesting and a good choice for a second career. She took a real estate course and passed the licensing exam. Carol now sells residential real estate. She loves her job, enjoys meeting new people and, of course, has additional income.

Position Description

Real Estate Professionals

Our housing market is sizzling! ABCX Realtors is expanding.
We want to bring onboard, energetic committed Real Estate
Associates who have the ambition and dedication to become the
best they can be, professionally!
If you have recently earned your Real Estate license or are
considering making a move from another firm, come see us!
We provide the best training and coaching in the industry to help
you succeed!
Our cutting-edge technology and marketing support are second
to none.

Qualifications

* _____ (State) Real Estate license
* Strong work ethic
* Energetic self starter
* Commitment to excellent customer service
* Enjoy networking and developing strong relationships
* Pleasant, can work independently or as a team member

ABCX Realtors has been in business for over 30 years and is a
full service brokerage. We are committed to the highest standards
of excellence and integrity. Our knowledgeable agents deliver
personal and responsive service which results in satisfied, repeat
customers.
Grow your career and join our team of real estate professionals.

We want to hear from you!
Call John Smith today at 111-222-3333.

CAROL

LinkedIn URL   email address   Cell

LICENSED NEW REAL ESTATE PROFESSIONAL

Energetic former educator ready for the challenge as a Real Estate Professional. Brings a stellar work ethic, excellent customer service and know-how and success in building relationships and networks. Experienced in hosting events and the use of social media to influence. Committed to customer satisfaction and providing the highest levels of professionalism.

PROFESSIONAL EXPERIENCE

SCHOOL, City, State   **20XX to 20XX**
Fifth Grade Teacher

Served as lead teacher in Art Magnet school with over 600 children in grades K - 5. Served as Art Department Chair for 10 years.

- Developed and implemented fundraising plan for Art Department, including school socials, social media and fun events
- Chaired, coordinated and performed as master of ceremonies for annual statewide continuing education programs for art educators.
- Chosen as a mentor for new teachers
- Served as sponsor for Art Club for 5 years winning district-wide Art Competition 3 years.
- As Art Department Chair, chosen as a judge for competitions in district

SCHOOL, Inner City, State   **20XX– 20XX**
First Grade Teacher

Taught First Grade serving the needs of a diverse population.

- Assessed each child's development level and created a process to meet individual needs.
- Oversaw teaching assistant while together creating a safe and playful classroom learning environment.

EDUCATION

BA, Education, University, City, State
XXX State Real Estate License
Mentor Training, 20XX

EXHIBIT D.3

Part-time Work, Receptionist at Veterinary Clinic

Mary, 60, had a career as a social services administrator which frequently included stress and accepting difficult realities. She felt overwhelmed. Mary took her retirement early and spent some time relaxing, playing with her two dogs and three cats in addition to reading and visiting with friends. No stress. She became restless and decided that a part-time job was the answer, preferably one dealing with her love of animals. When Mary saw a part-time receptionist job posting at the clinic where she took her own pets, she applied. Mary was overqualified for this position. She convinced the clinic manager that after her short-lived retirement, she was ready and eager to work with her favorite creatures—animals—and the public. The manager hired Mary and she now works a three-day week with occasional weekends—the perfect job for her.

Position Description

Veterinary Clinic Front Desk (Part-time)

Will train the right person for this position

Our clinic is a friendly place to work where we strive to make both our employees and customers feel like family.
We have a part-time opening for a very nice, efficient person to run our front desk.
We are looking for an animal lover with a sunny personality, who will interact with our furry friends, their owners and our veterinarians.

Duties:
- Greet clients and answer their questions
- Answer phones
- Schedule appointments
- **Check pets in and out**
- Collect client fees
- Manage computerized medical records.

Qualifications:
- Ardent animal lover
- Cheerful and sunny personality
- Dependable
- Excellent customer service
- Computer experience
- Detail-oriented
- Team player
- Able to work some weekends
- Minimum Age 18

If you are interested, please speak to Leona at 000-111-2222.

MARY

City, State

| LinkedIn URL | Email Address | Cell |

PROFILE

Cheerful professional looking for new "work home" to combine customer service skills, computer competencies and love of animals. Known for efficiency, dependability and being a team player. Enjoys working with people and pets. Can work flexible hours and available to work some weekends.

PROFESSIONAL EXPERIENCE

ASSISTED LIVING CENTER, City, State   **20XX – 20XX**
Director, Resident Care
On call 24/7 to direct and coordinate nursing care for 100 chronically ill seniors. Educated staff in relating to family and patients. Built lines of communication between patient, family members, staff and administration to build and retain customer base and improve employee retention. Provided on-going nursing and direct care, including medication management and referrals for positive patient outcomes. Wrote policies and procedures and monitored for compliance. Implemented and trained staff on usage of new computer records system.

CARE FACILITY, City, State   **20XX – 20XX**
Director
Collaborated with multiple interdisciplinary teams for effective patient care outcomes, favorable public relations and new referrals. Wrote and updated policy and procedures. Maintained high standards with JCAHO (citation-free) and state accreditation. Conducted monthly Alzheimer's community support group meetings, doubling membership. Opened lines of communication by instituting and facilitating weekly team meetings.

EDUCATION

MS, Social Work, University, City, State
BS, Nursing, University, City, State

113

EXHIBIT D.4

Entrepreneur, Wedding Planner

June, 65, had worked as a Project Coordinator for a large pharmaceutical company. She was responsible for planning corporate events and conferences. June's flair and attention to detail earned her many commendations. After retirement, she and her husband traveled extensively. June also volunteered at the nearby hospital.

Her niece became engaged and asked June to help plan her wedding which was only three months away. With her well-honed expertise, she created a lovely, memorable event which impressed several guests. Before June knew it, she received calls for her services. As a favor, she coordinated several weddings. Her reputation grew and the phone calls increased. June soon had people asking her to help with a variety of events. One of the hospitals hired her to plan their donor appreciation dinner. June decided to become an accredited wedding and event planner. She realizes that her corporate experience has turned into a small, profitable business.

Entrepreneur, Physical Trainer

Bill, 66, was a procurement logistics professional in the chemical industry. He had always been passionate about exercise and worked out five times a week at the local gym. He became buddies with several of the trainers who encouraged his commitment to physical fitness. Bill was laid-off at age 64. At first, he was depressed. After speaking with his financial planner, he realized his financial portfolio was ample and he could do whatever he wanted. With this in mind, Bill decided to pursue his love of physical fitness and help others become fit. He became a certified physical trainer. Using his contacts within the fitness community, Bill markets his services to mature adults and, by choice, works twenty hours a week. He gains a great sense of satisfaction by turning couch potatoes into more active adults.

Business Plan Considerations

Following a detailed business plan is essential to the success of your business, whether it is relatively low-cost or involving significant financial investment. Research the numerous resources for business plan samples and templates available on the internet.

The following components should be included in your business plan.

- What type of business are you starting?
- Do you have the skills and certifications necessary for this business?
- Will you work alone or have partners?
- What is the realistic market for your business?
- What are your goals?
- How are your competitors doing?
- What will you offer that will differentiate your business from your competitors?
- What are your strategies?
- Do you have a supportive network?
- What are your startup costs?
  - business/tax setup
  - liability insurance
  - computer system
  - appropriate software

- specialty services—bookkeeping, computer tech support, etc.
- office equipment
- office supplies
- social media accounts
- professional website
- marketing, advertising costs
- networking costs
- miscellaneous

- What is your budget?

- Do you need financing?

- Where will you get it?

- Can you afford to lose your investment?

- Where and how do you find customers?

- How much should you charge?

- What is the revenue range for this type of business?

- How long will it take your business to break even and to be profitable?

- Do you have the resources and endurance to reach business profitability?

- How and when will you consider your business to be a success or not?

- What is your exit strategy?

EXHIBIT D.5

Consultant, Human Resources Project Work

Ann, 62, was a Human Resources professional with a career spanning more than 30 years. She had a wide variety of experience, including employee recruitment, performance management, training and diversity initiatives. Ann was laid off following her firm's acquisition by a larger company. With her partner of many years, she traveled to a second home in another state and began her retirement. After six months, Ann decided to explore contract work options. By working with a Human Resources Consulting firm, Ann is able to find enough work for six months out of the year which is exactly what she wants.

Position Description

Human Resource Professionals
Full-time, Part-time, Project Work

pCHRM is an industry leader in providing outsourced Human Resources professionals for small and midsized businesses. We currently have several opportunities for proven Human Resources Professionals (HRPs) to join our team in varying capacities.

We provide our clients with part-time and full-time HR experts on a flexible, project or on a regularly scheduled basis. If you are interested in providing your HR expertise to assist client business during peak periods or special projects; or provide interim HR direction and consulting services.

This position will be the ideal opportunity for you!

We are looking for HRPs (managers and directors) who can jump in to help clients to achieve their HR goals.

Required Experience:
- Recruit employees that fit company's business goals and culture
- Review and strengthen retention program
- Provide staff training and development
- Implement diversity awareness program
- Monitor Affirmative Action and EEO compliance
- Create processes and strategies to comply with ADA and FMLA changes
- Develop and implement process improvement policies
- Help newer HR professionals get up to speed faster by mentoring
- Assist clients with whatever HR expertise is required

Credentials:
- Bachelor's Degree
- Graduate Degree with specialization in Human Resources preferred
- PHR or SPHR Certification
- 10-plus years Human Resources experience

Please submit your resume online www.PCHRM.com

ANN
City, State

LinkedIn URL	Email Address	Cell

HUMAN RESOURCES CONSULTANT

Human Resources professional with extensive experience in employee recruitment as well as training and development. Expertise in creating programs that increase employee productivity. Highly effective in motivating and directing employees. Exceptional interpersonal and written communications skills.

EXPERTISE

- Recruitment and Selection
- Training and Development
- Affirmative Action and EEO
- Diversity Awareness
- ADA and FMLA
- Employee Communications
- Performance Management
- Mentoring

SELECTED ACCOMPLISHMENTS

Human Resources Administration

- Successfully recruited hard-to-find special skills employees that helped expand company businesses.
- Established diversity recruiting and awareness program that broadened company's employee base.
- Brought Affirmative Action and EEO to compliance
- Implemented strategies to comply with ADA and FMLA.
- Created positive employee relations environment through development of employee newsletter and ongoing employee communication programs.
- As member of process improvement team, wrote, updated and implemented policy procedures for all U.S. and international locations resulting in clear, easily understood and consistently applied policies, procedures and guidelines.

Training and Development

- Developed and delivered training programs for management, service and sales staff resulting in 6% reduction in customer service complaints.
- Established mentoring program for executives that created a teamwork environment.

ANN   **PAGE TWO**

- Directed completion of quality assessments, along with compilation and analysis of results, ensuring that new program administration was consistent with corporate strategic goals.
- Designed and implemented multi-purpose orientation program for newly hired employees achieving 40% increase in employee retention.

Management and Supervision

- Led team in the development of national express service program representing 45% of all business transactions and resulting in a 5% market share increase.
- Maintained staff productivity and commitment to quality by encouraging involvement in process improvements by implementing applicable suggestions as well as recognizing employee contributions.
- Received Award for successful mentoring program for high potential employees.

PROFESSIONAL EXPERIENCE

COMPANY #1 City, State   20XX– 20XX
Director, Human Resources
Senior Manager, Human Resources
Manager, Human Resources

COMPANY #2, City, State   **20XX– 20XX**
Customer Services Manager
Customer Services Representative

EDUCATION

B.A., Psychology
University, City, State

M.S. Human Resources Management
University, City, State

SPHR Certification 20XX

PROFESSIONAL ASSOCIATIONS

Human Resources Association (HRA)
Society of Human Resources Managers (SHRM)

EXHIBIT D.6

Volunteer, Certified Visiting Pets Program

Jack, 67, was ready to retire from his career in retail. His knees and back hurt. Jack wanted to take care of his health and spend time with the family, especially his grandchildren. He soon discovered that his grandchildren had their own schedules and commitments. Jack had plenty of free time available. At first, he thought about returning to work on a part-time basis, but decided that he needed something new to do. Jack began to investigate volunteering and discovered that he and his dog, Jupiter, could volunteer together. He had Jupiter trained and certified as a therapy dog. Together, they now visit nursing homes. Jack loves bringing a bit of joy to the infirm and elderly.

Position Description

Volunteer Opportunity

- WANTED: Certified Visiting Pets for XXXX Assisted Living Center Visits
- LOCATION: XXXX Assisted Living Centers
- WHEN: It's flexible! We'll work with your schedule.
- WHERE: Large U.S. cities
- ABOUT: Volunteer with therapy pet for visits to XXXX Assisted Living Centers
- ABOUT: XXXX Assisted Living Centers understands the transformative powers of simply snuggling a dog or cat. That is why we are seeking individuals who have certified visiting pets to visit people living in XXXX Assisted Living Centers. As a volunteer with a certified visiting pet, you will bring a connection and care to our seniors who could use a bit of extra attention. Let your pet be a bridge to share a smile. Volunteer training is free—times and locations are flexible. Contact Mary Smith, Volunteer Coordinator, for more details.
- GOOD MATCH FOR: Retirees

Requirements and Commitment:

- Driver's License Needed
- Background Check
- Must be at least 18 years old
- Orientation or Training
- Flexible; commitment of 2–6 hours per week
- Certification documents for visiting pets
- Prefer volunteer experience but not essential

LETTER OF INTEREST

VOLUNTEER POSITION
CERTIFIED VISITING PETS PROGRAM

Dear _____.

I am very interested in the volunteer position for an individual with a certified therapy dog. I noticed the advertisement listed on your website. It immediately caught my attention as I have interest in helping the senior community.

My dog, Jupiter has been trained and certified as a Therapy Dog. We are both ready to bring a bit of joy to those who can benefit from the sweetest dog ever.

I am a retiree who enjoyed a long career in retail especially interacting with my many customers. I have volunteered as a hospital buddy and would also love to visit seniors with my dog. My schedule is flexible and I will be available to take your training/orientation class.

Per your website information, I will call _____ to set up an appointment.

I look forward to being of service to my community

Sincerely,
Jack Smith
Email
Cell Phone

About the Authors

**TOBY
HABERKORN**

Toby Haberkorn is an experienced executive-search consultant and certified job search strategist. She enjoys working with mature individuals who are at crossroads in their careers and lives. Toby is known for her job-market knowledge, strategic expertise, and mentoring. She helps individuals determine and achieve their goals.

Toby's career has ranged from being the Executive Director of a Cultural Arts Center to working in Human Resources Management and retained-executive search as well as having written an industrial newsletter.

She earned a Bachelor's degree in History from Case Western Reserve University in Cleveland, Ohio, and a Master's degree in Human Resources Management from the University of Houston in Houston, Texas. Toby is also the author of two children's books.

**ELIZABETH
O'NEAL**

Elizabeth is a career coach who supports individuals in career transition and those who are just exploring their options. She brings energy and enthusiasm to workshops and presentations.

Elizabeth is passionate about helping people manage their transition and especially enjoys assisting candidates who are considering career changes or retirement to explore options.

With a background in the financial service industry, she is a career consultant with a global career and talent development firm. Elizabeth earned a Bachelor of Science in Economics from Texas A&M University in College Station, Texas.

Made in the USA
Columbia, SC
04 December 2020